C000101622

A-level
Success

Biology

AQA

Practice Test Papers

Tom Adams

Contents

ACKNOWLEDGEMENTS

The author and publisher are grateful to the copyright holders for permission to use quoted materials and images.

Cover & P1: © tr3gin/Shutterstock.com

P9: fig 4 - TEM Microscape/Science Photo Library;
P11: fig 5 - Steve Gschmeissner/Science Photo Library;
P46: fig 10 - Skinner M, et al. Epigenetics and the Evolution of Darwin's Finches. Genome Biology and Evolution Vol 6 (8), 2014: 1972-1989, by permission of Oxford University Press;
P61: fig 7 - Thompson RC, et al. Lost at Sea: Where Is All the Plastic? Science Vol 304 (5672) pp. 838, 2004, by permission of The American Association for the Advancement of Science

All other images are © Shutterstock.com & © HarperCollins*Publishers* Ltd

Every effort has been made to trace copyright holders and obtain their permission for the use of copyright material. The author and publisher will gladly receive information enabling them to rectify any error or omission in subsequent editions. All facts are correct at time of going to press.

Published by Letts Educational
An imprint of HarperCollins*Publishers*
1 London Bridge Street
London SE1 9GF

ISBN: 9780008179014

First published 2016

10 9 8 7 6 5 4 3 2 1

© HarperCollins*Publishers* Limited 2016

All rights reserved. No part of this publication may be reproduced, stored in a retrieval system, or transmitted, in any form or by any means, electronic, mechanical, photocopying, recording or otherwise, without the prior permission of Letts Educational.

British Library Cataloguing in Publication Data.
A CIP record of this book is available from the British Library.

Series Concept and Development: Emily Linnett and Katherine Wilkinson
Author: Tom Adams
Commissioning and Series Editor: Chantal Addy
Editorial: Jill Laidlaw
Cover Design: Paul Oates
Inside Concept Design: Ian Wrigley
Text Design and Layout: Aptara®, inc.
Production: Lyndsey Rogers
Printed in China

MIX
Paper from responsible sources
FSC™ C007454

A-level
Biology
Practice paper for AQA

Paper 1

Time allowed: 2 hours

> **Materials**
> For this paper you must have:
> - a ruler with millimetre measurements
> - a calculator.

Instructions
- Use black ink or black ball-point pen.
- Fill in the box at the bottom of this page.
- Answer **all** questions.

Information
- The marks for questions are shown in brackets.
- The maximum mark for this paper is 91.

Name: ....

Answer **all** questions in the spaces provided.

0 1 **Figure 1** shows the structure of a fibrous protein called collagen.

Figure 1

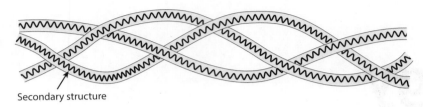

Secondary structure

The secondary structure of the protein is shown in the fibres.

0 1 · 1 State the name of this type of secondary structure.

[1 mark]

Collagen is rich in the amino acids proline and glycine. The structure of these molecules is shown in **Figure 2**. They can join together to form a peptide bond.

Figure 2

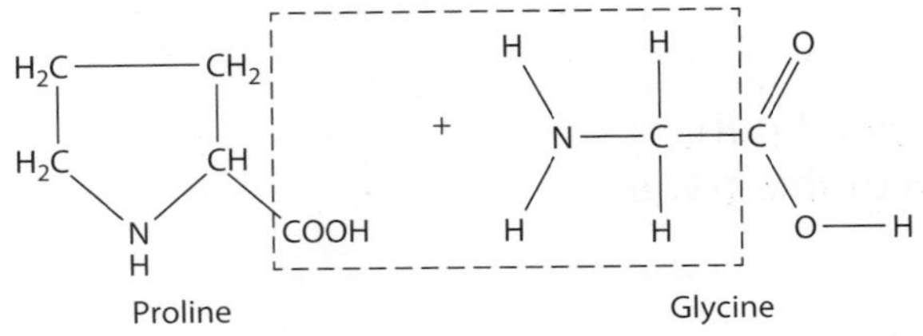

H_2C——CH_2

H_2C CH

N COOH
H

Proline

+

H   H   O

N——C——C

H   H   O——H

Glycine

0 1 · 2 Which smaller molecule is eliminated in this reaction?

[1 mark]

0 1 · 3 Draw a ring round the R group of the glycine molecule.

[1 mark]

0 1 . 4 In the space below, draw the chemical bond formed when these two amino acids are joined together. Only draw the portions of the molecule **within** the box in **Figure 2**.

[2 marks]

0 1 . 5 Collagen is a tissue found in tendons, which join muscles to bones. Explain how collagen's structure is adapted for this function.

[2 marks]

....

....

0 2 Albumen is a **globular** protein found in egg white. When heated, the protein changes from a transparent appearance to opaque white.

0 2 · 1 What name is given to this change?

[1 mark]

....

0 2 · 2 Explain how a raised temperature can change the tertiary structure of albumen.

[3 marks]

....

....

....

....

0 2 · 3 Describe how you would carry out a biochemical test to determine that albumen was indeed a protein.

[2 marks]

....

....

....

0 2 · 4 During digestion, long-chain polypeptides are hydrolysed to smaller molecules that can be absorbed across cell membranes.

Compare and contrast how endopeptidases and exopeptidases break down these polypeptide molecules.

[3 marks]

....

....

....

....

0 3 Invertase is a yeast-derived enzyme that splits **sucrose** into **glucose** and **fructose**. Invertase can be used to produce liquefied centres in creams, truffles and other confections. Sucrose crystallises more easily than fructose and glucose.

Figure 3

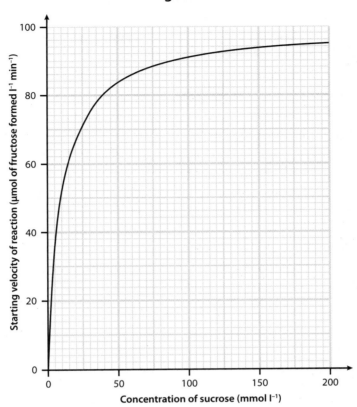

0 3 · 1 Which concentration of sucrose causes a reaction starting velocity of 70 μmol of fructose $l^{-1}min^{-1}$?

[1 mark]

.... mmol l^{-1}

0 3 · 2 For each of the control variables below, suggest **how** they could be controlled.

[1 mark]

Temperature ....

[1 mark]

pH ....

0 3 · 3 Explain how invertase might increase the shelf life of confections.

[2 marks]

....

....

0 3 . 4 The yeast from which invertase is extracted is a strain called *Saccharomyces cerevisiae*. Complete **Table 1** to show its classification.

[2 marks]

Table 1

Taxon	Name of Taxon
Domain	
Kingdom	Fungi
	Ascomycota
Class	Saccharomycetes
	Saccharomycetales
Family	Saccharomycetaceae

0 4 **Figure 4** shows a transmission electron micrograph of a macrophage cell. The micrograph has been magnified **6000** times.

Figure 4

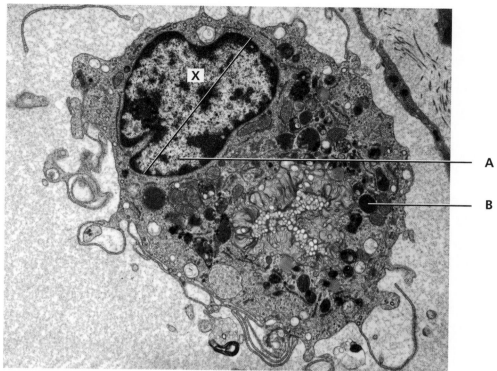

0 4 . **1** Give the name and function of structure **A**.

[1 mark]

Name of **A** ....

Function of **A** ....

0 4 . **2** Structure **B** is a lysosome. Explain why this cell has a large number of these organelles.

[2 marks]

....

....

0 4 . **3** Measure the apparent diameter of structure **A** along the line indicated by an **X** in **Figure 4**.

Calculate the **actual** diameter of structure **A in** μm using the information given.

[2 marks]

Actual diameter of **X** ....

0 5 . 1 Describe how you would prepare a specimen of stained squashes of cells from plant root tips such as garlic or onion for observation under a light microscope. You should name a suitable stain in your answer.

[5 marks]

_____

_____

_____

_____

_____

_____

_____

_____

_____

_____

_____

[Extra space] _____

_____

_____

_____

_____

Figure 5 shows a view of a cell squash specimen taken from an onion root tip.

Figure 5

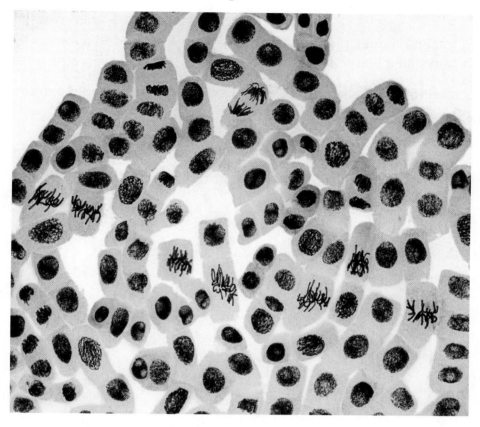

0 5 · 2 Count the number of cells that are actively undergoing metaphase or anaphase (where the chromosomes can be clearly seen).

[No marks for this]

Number _____

Assuming there are 130 cells in this field of view, calculate the **mitotic index** of the specimen.

[2 marks]

Answer _____ %

0 6   The following experiment was carried out to investigate **plasmolysis** in plant cells.

- A strip of epidermis from the inner surface of a red onion's fleshy storage leaves was peeled away.

- Using forceps, a small piece of epidermis was transferred to a microscope slide and three drops of distilled water added.

- After placing a coverslip on top, the cells were examined under a microscope.

Figure 6 shows the appearance of the cells.

Figure 6

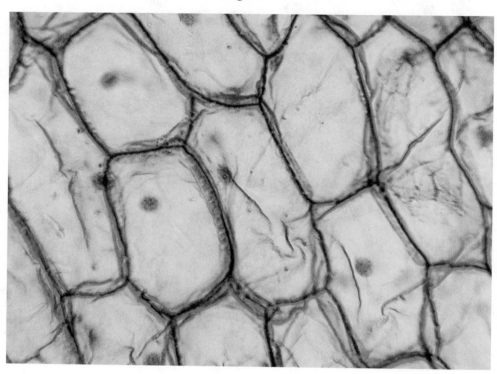

The procedure was repeated, but this time the epidermis was mounted in 1 M sucrose solution. Many of the cells had a different appearance. They had been **plasmolysed**.

0 6 . 1   In the space below, draw the likely appearance of a single cell placed in 1 M sucrose solution. Label the cytoplasm.

[2 marks]

0 6 . 2 Plasmolysis rarely occurs in nature. However, plants that live in salt marshes have to resist plasmolysis. Explain, in terms of water potential, why this is so.

[2 marks]

_____

_____

_____

0 6 . 3 Suggest a reason for using red onion rather than white onion for the experiment.

[1 mark]

_____

_____

A plant scientist counted the number of cells she could see in the microscope's field of view. She also counted the total number of cells.

She then set up different slides where onion cells were mounted in a range of different concentrations of sucrose solution. Her results are shown in **Table 2**.

Table 2

Concentration of sucrose solution/M	Number of plasmolysed cells	Total number of cells	% plasmolysed cells
0.05	0	40	0.0
0.15	2	57	3.5
0.25	5	48	
0.35	32	50	64.0
0.45	50	64	78.1
0.55	50	50	100

0 6 . 4 Calculate the percentage of plasmolysed onion cells in 0.25 M sucrose solution.

[1 mark]

.... %

0 6 · 5 Use **Figure 7** to draw a graph to display these results. The axes have been labelled for you.

[3 marks]

Figure 7

When the contents of a plant cell are isotonic with the external solution, a state of **incipient plasmolysis** is the result. This is the concentration where cytoplasm is just held in place against the cell wall. Experimentally, this can be estimated by finding the external concentration that results in 50% of cells being plasmolysed. Thus, you can find the concentration of the cell's sap.

0 6 · 6 Draw two lines on your graph to show the data values at incipient plasmolysis. Use your graph to estimate the concentration of cell sap in red onion leaf cells.

[2 marks]

0 7 **Figure 8** shows how the metabolic rates of various mammals change with their body mass.

Figure 8

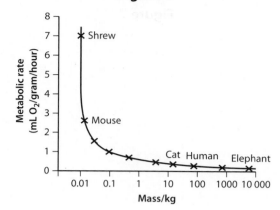

0 7 · 1 The body mass is plotted on a non-linear scale. Suggest why the data was presented this way.

[1 mark]

0 7 · 2 Describe and explain the relationship between metabolic rate per gram per hour and body mass.

[3 marks]

0 7 · 3 Smaller organisms, such as the protist amoeba, have no special tissues, organs or systems for gaseous exchange. Mammals are large, multicellular organisms and have more complex systems.

Explain why mammals need such systems whereas single-celled organisms do not.

[2 marks]

| 0 | 8 | **Figure 9** shows the pressure changes that occur in the human heart.

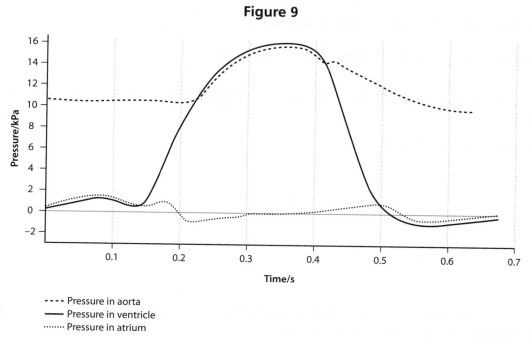

Figure 9

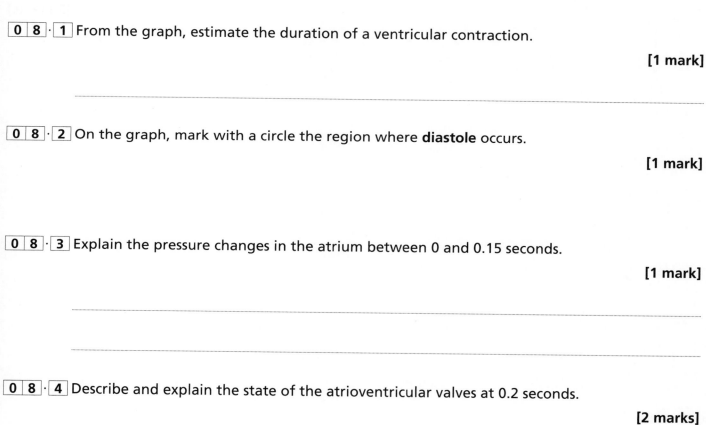

| 0 | 8 | · | 1 | From the graph, estimate the duration of a ventricular contraction.

[1 mark]

| 0 | 8 | · | 2 | On the graph, mark with a circle the region where **diastole** occurs.

[1 mark]

| 0 | 8 | · | 3 | Explain the pressure changes in the atrium between 0 and 0.15 seconds.

[1 mark]

| 0 | 8 | · | 4 | Describe and explain the state of the atrioventricular valves at 0.2 seconds.

[2 marks]

0 8 . 5 Cardiac output can be calculated using the formula:

Cardiac output = stroke volume × heart rate

Litres per minute   litres per beat   beats per minute

The resting cardiac output of an athlete is 7.15 litres per minute at a heart rate of 65 beats per minute.

Calculate the stroke volume.

[2 marks]

.... litres

0 8 . 6 After training, the maximum heart rate of an athlete increases by 20 bpm. Explain the advantage of this increase to an athlete.

[3 marks]

....

....

....

....

....

0 9   **Haemoglobin** is a protein found in a wide range of organisms. It can reversibly combine with oxygen to form **oxyhaemoglobin**.

Figure 10 shows the oxygen dissociation curve for human haemoglobin at a range of partial pressures.

Figure 10

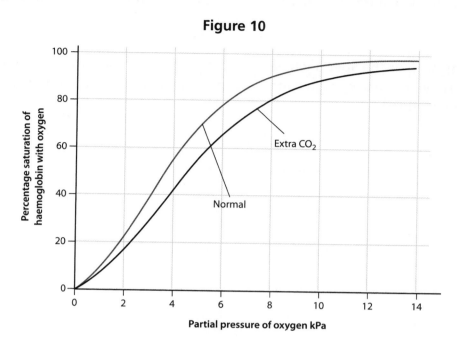

0 9 . 1 In the lungs, the partial pressure of oxygen can be as high as 14 kPa. Explain how haemoglobin's properties are an advantage in this situation.

[2 marks]

....

....

....

....

0 9 . 2 Explain the effect on the oxygen dissociation curve of a high partial pressure of carbon dioxide at a muscle.

[2 marks]

....

....

....

....

Another protein that acts in a similar way to haemoglobin is **myoglobin**. **Myoglobin** does not travel in the blood but is found in muscle. It has a greater affinity for oxygen than haemoglobin.

0 9 . 3 Draw a curve on **Figure 10** to show the oxygen dissociation curve for myoglobin.

[1 mark]

0 9 . 4 Cetaceans, such as the Sperm whale, dive beneath the ocean surface for long periods of time. They have a very high concentration of myoglobin in their muscles. Explain the advantage of this.

[2 marks]

....

....

....

....

In the past, farmers were given a subsidy to 'set aside' land previously used for arable farming to encourage the development of natural habitats for a greater range of wildlife. No cultivation was carried out on land set aside in this manner.

Scientists investigated the biodiversity of two equally-sized plots of neighbouring land on a certain farm. One area – **Plot A**, had been set aside for **five** years. The other area – **Plot B**, had been set aside for only **two** years. They used small quadrats of side 0.25 m to sample the two plots and collected data showing the number and range of plant species. Plants were individually counted within the quadrat.

Selected results are shown in **Table 3**.

Table 3

Plant species	Mean number of species per quadrat		P value
	Plot A	Plot B	
Common bent	18	2	0.015
Wavy hairgrass	10	25	0.025
Buck's-horn plantain	1	5	0.010
Heath speedwell	0	3	0.001
Rosebay willow herb	11	3	0.067
Harebell	1	3	0.020
Thistle	5	1	0.015

Species diversity is given as:

$$d = \frac{N(N-1)}{\Sigma n(n-1)}$$

where N = total number of organisms of all species

and n = total number of organisms of each species.

1 0 . 1 Calculate the species diversity for **Plot A** and **Plot B**.

[2 marks]

Plot A species diversity ....

Plot B species diversity ....

1 0 . 2 Suggest reasons for the difference between these two indices.

[2 marks]

....

....

....

....

1 0 . 3 A statistical test was carried out that enabled the scientists to see if the difference in number between **Plot A** and **Plot B** of each species was significant or not. The **P values** obtained are shown in **Table 3**.

Explain the conclusions that can be drawn from this analysis.

[3 marks]

....

....

....

....

....

....

....

1 1 Describe the structure and function of the molecule ATP.

[5 marks]

[Extra space]

1 2 Compare and contrast the processes of **transpiration** and **translocation** in a plant.

[6 marks]

....

....

....

....

....

....

....

....

....

[Extra space] ....

....

....

....

....

....

....

1 3 Describe and explain the uses of vaccines in protecting **individuals** and **populations**.

[4 marks]

....

....

....

....

....

....

....

....

[Extra space] ....

....

....

....

....

....

....

....

END OF QUESTIONS

A-level
Biology
Practice paper for AQA

Paper 2

Time allowed: 2 hours

> **Materials**
> For this paper you must have:
> - a ruler with millimetre measurements
> - a calculator.

Instructions
- Use black ink or black ball-point pen.
- Fill in the box at the bottom of this page.
- Answer **all** questions.

Information
- The marks for questions are shown in brackets.
- The maximum mark for this paper is 91.

Name: ....

Scientists recreated Calvin's classic experiment to investigate the biochemical pathway of the light-independent reaction.

Figure 1 shows the apparatus used.

Figure 1

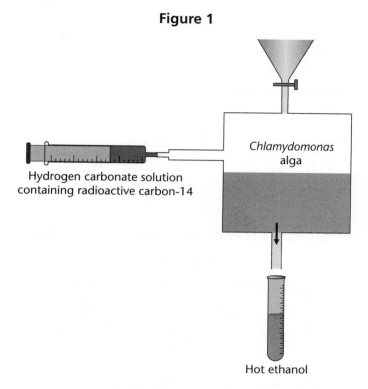

Hot ethanol

The apparatus was placed in a darkened room and the *Chlamydomonas* alga given radioactive carbon-14. The contents of the tank were then mixed and a bright light switched on. Every five seconds, *Chlamydomonas* cells were extracted and put into hot ethanol. The cells were then homogenised (mashed up to form a liquid) and the process of two-way chromatography carried out. This involved performing chromatography with one solvent running, then turning the chromatogram through 90° and running it again with a different solvent. The separated substances had no colour, but the scientists were able to detect the compounds by exposing the chromatogram to a photographic plate. Radioactive compounds were revealed where the plate 'fogged' over.

0 1 · 1 Why was carbonate solution introduced into the apparatus?

[1 mark]

....

....

0 1 . 2 Why were the algae poured into hot ethanol?

[1 mark]

....

....

0 1 . 3 Explain why the cells were homogenised.

[1 mark]

....

....

Figure 2 shows the results of the two-way chromatography analysis.

Figure 2

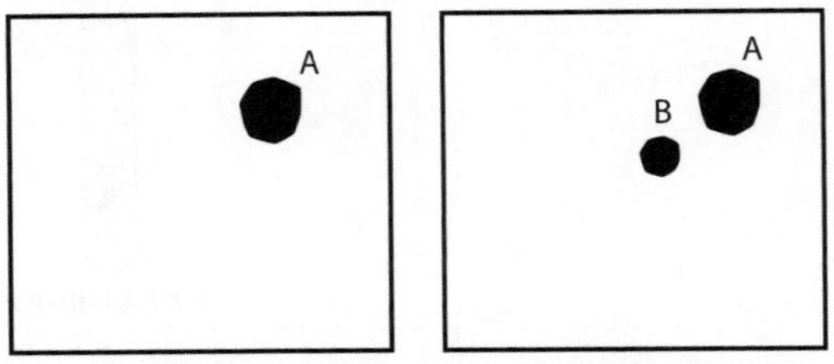

After 5 seconds   After 10 seconds

0 1 . 4 Using what you know of the light-independent stage of photosynthesis, suggest names for compounds **A** and **B**.

[2 marks]

A ....

B ....

Another experiment was carried out to determine the quantities of two compounds produced during the light-independent reaction. The experiment consisted of a light and then a dark regime. **Figure 3** shows a graph of the results obtained.

Figure 3

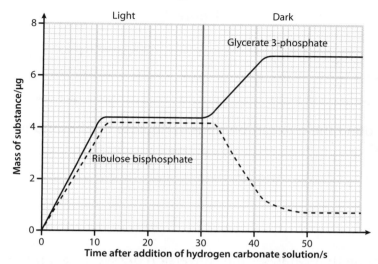

0 1 . 5 Calculate the percentage increase in glycerate 3-phosphate between 30 and 43 seconds to one decimal place.

[2 marks]

.... %

0 1 . 6 Explain why the levels of glycerate 3-phosphate increase then level out after the light is switched off.

[2 marks]

....

....

....

0 1 . 7 Explain why levels of ribulose bisphosphate decrease.

[2 marks]

....

....

Immediately as the radioactive carbon was introduced, the research team analysed the glycerate 3-phosphate. They found that the carbon ring labelled 'R' was radioactive.

Figure 4 shows the structure of glycerate 3-phosphate and the ribulose bisphosphate formed from it.

Figure 4

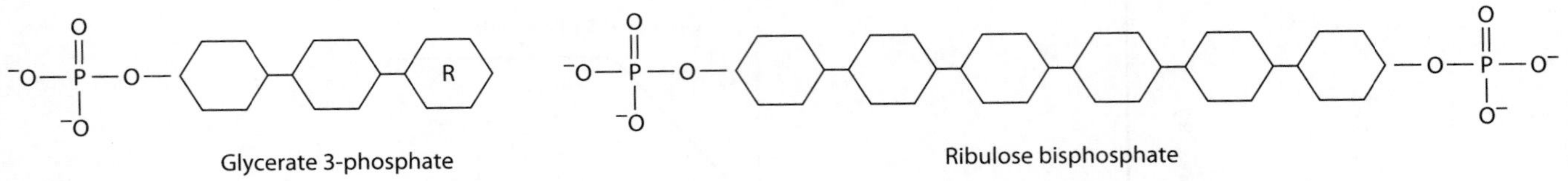

Glycerate 3-phosphate   Ribulose bisphosphate

0 1 . 8 | Draw a circle round the two carbon rings in ribulose bisphosphate that are likely to be radioactive.

[1 mark]

0 1 . 9 | Name the enzyme that catalyses the conversion of glycerate 3-phosphate to ribulose bisphosphate.

[1 mark]

Figure 5 shows the main stages of the nitrogen cycle.

Figure 5

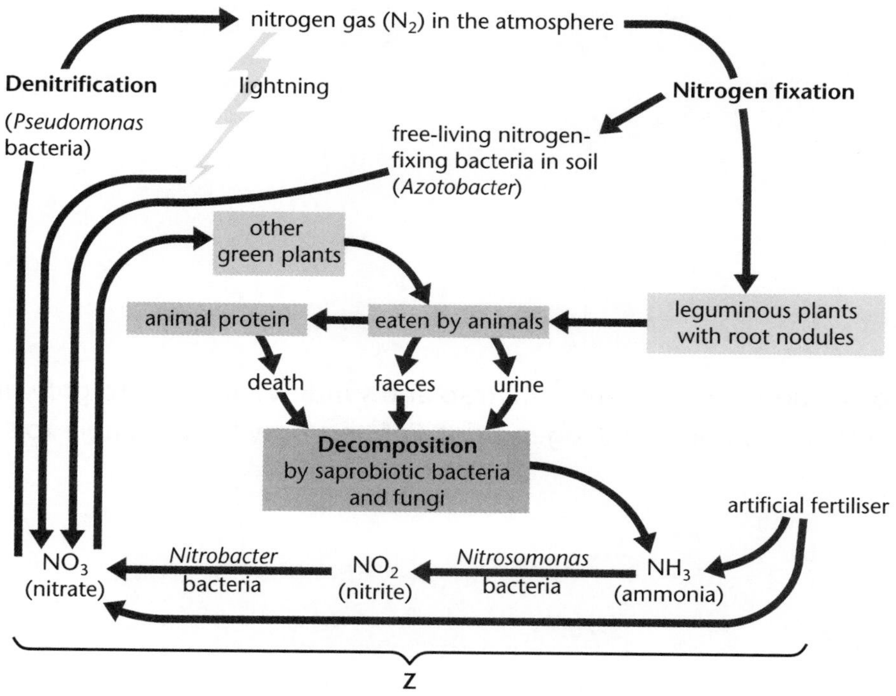

0 2 . 1 Process Z includes the reactions that convert ammonia to nitrate. What is the name of this process?

[1 mark]

0 2 . 2 In nitrogen fixation, bacteria such as *Rhizobium* make use of atmospheric nitrogen to make it available for leguminous plants to use. Describe this process, stating the ion initially formed and the compounds in the plant requiring the nitrogen.

[2 marks]

0 2 . 3 Waterlogged soil is very oxygen-poor. Explain, using your knowledge of denitrification, why such soil also has low concentrations of **nitrate**.

[2 marks]

_____

_____

_____

_____

0 2 . 4 Carnivorous plants such as Venus's flytrap and sundews are able to grow in swamps and bogs despite the soil being nitrogen-poor. Suggest how they are able to survive.

[2 marks]

_____

_____

_____

0 2 . 5 As well as nitrate, phosphate is an important mineral ion required by plants. Farmers apply fertilisers that contain high concentrations of nitrate and phosphate to fields. When it rains, some of this fertiliser can run off into nearby rivers.

Why do plants require phosphate for healthy growth?

[1 mark]

_____

_____

Scientists sampled the water in seven rivers and streams within the same county. They measured the concentration of phosphates in the water of each river and the mass of algal cells present. Their data are shown in **Table 1**.

Table 1

River	Phosphate concentration gl^{-1} (x)	Algal concentration µg l^{-1} (y)	xy	x^2	y^2
A	343	462	158 466	117 649	213 444
B	198	227	44 946	39 204	51 529
C	317	407	129 019	100 489	165 649
D	243	374	90 882	59 049	139 876
E	161	222	35 742	25 921	49 284
F	193	375	72 375	37 249	140 625
G	195	230	44 850	38 025	52 900
Σ	1650	2297	576 280	417 586	813 307

The table also shows the totals needed in order to calculate a correlation coefficient.

0 2 · 6 Calculate the **correlation coefficient** (r) for this data using the formula below:

$$r = \frac{n(\Sigma xy) - (\Sigma x)(\Sigma y)}{\sqrt{[n\Sigma x^2 - (\Sigma x)^2][n\Sigma y^2 - (\Sigma y)^2]}}$$

where **n** is the sample size (i.e. 7).

Use the space below to show your working.

[3 marks]

r = ...

0 2 . 7 The scientists concluded that increased phosphate concentrations were causing an increased quantity of algae in the waterways. Do you agree with them? Explain your response.

[1 mark]

Decision (agree/disagree) _____

Explanation _____

_____

_____

0 2 . 8 The addition of phosphate to waterways can cause **eutrophication**. Describe how this type of pollution harms aquatic habitats.

[3 marks]

_____

_____

_____

_____

_____

_____

The choice chamber in **Figure 6** can be used to investigate the behaviour of the crustacean woodlouse *Armadillidium* and their preference for dark or light conditions.

Figure 6

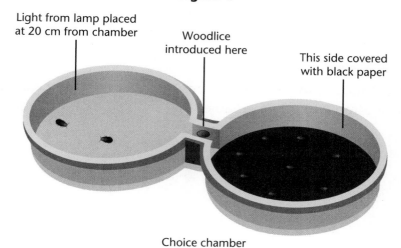

Choice chamber

- One side is darkened by covering and securing it with tape, the other is left exposed to a source of artificial light.

- Ten woodlice are introduced to the centre of the choice chamber and the lid is replaced.

- After 5 minutes the number of woodlice are counted in the exposed half. This number is subtracted from the total to find the number of woodlice in the dark half.

- The whole process is repeated 10 times.

Some data from the experiment are shown in **Table 2**.

Table 2

Trial	Woodlice count after 5 minutes	
	In the light	In the dark
1	2	8
2	4	6
3	3	7
4	4	6
5	3	7
6	4	6
7	5	5
8	6	4
9	3	7
10	5	5
Totals		

0 3 · 1 State a suitable null hypothesis for this experiment.

[1 mark]

....

....

0 3 · 2 The students conducting the experiment ensured that they used woodlice of the same species and size. State **two** other variables that should be controlled.

[2 marks]

Variable 1 ....

Variable 2 ....

0 3 · 3 A chi-squared analysis can be carried out to find out whether there are any significant differences shown in the woodlice distribution. Use the experimental data in **Table 2** along with **Table 3** and the formula below to calculate a value of chi-squared.

Table 3

	Light	Dark
Observed results (O)		
Expected results (E)		
$(O–E)^2$		
$(O–E)^2/E$		

$$\chi^2 = \sum \frac{(O - E)^2}{E}$$

O = the frequencies observed
E = the frequencies expected
$\sum$ = the 'sum of'

[3 marks]

$\chi^2 =$ ....

$\boxed{0\ 3}\cdot\boxed{4}$ The students concluded that woodlice show a definite preference for dark conditions. **Table 4** shows critical values. Use **Table 4** to comment on the students' findings.

[2 marks]

Table 4

Degrees of freedom	Critical value for 95% confidence
1	3.84
2	5.99
3	7.82
4	9.49
5	11.07
6	12.59
7	14.07
8	15.51
9	16.92
10	18.31

Degrees of freedom = number of categories (N) − 1

....

....

....

$\boxed{0\ 3}\cdot\boxed{5}$ Woodlice also exhibit responses to tactile (touch) stimuli. They are said to show a negative taxis to touch. Explain what this term means.

[2 marks]

....

....

Dihybrid inheritance refers to genetic crosses for genes at different loci (positions) on chromosomes. In pea plants, the colour and texture of seeds are determined by two genes at different loci. Letters are given to the various genes as follows:

R = round seeds (dominant)   r = wrinkled seeds (recessive)

Y = yellow seeds (dominant)   y = green seeds (recessive)

A cross was carried out by a gardener where a heterozygous pea plant for both traits was pollinated by another heterozygous plant. The gardener took the seeds from this cross and counted the number of each type. Her results are shown in **Table 5**.

Table 5

Seed description	Number
Round and yellow	217
Round and green	80
Wrinkled and yellow	66
Wrinkled and green	22

0 4 . 1 Use the genetic cross framework below to show how these progeny could have resulted.

Gametes produced by each parent plant:

....

[1 mark]

[2 marks]

0 4 . 2 What ratio would you expect for the seed genotypes in this cross?

[1 mark]

0 4 . 3 Give **two** reasons why the actual numbers obtained from dihybrid crosses may vary from the expected numbers.

[2 marks]

....

....

Figure 7 shows the family tree of a family where some progeny have the condition haemophilia.

Figure 7

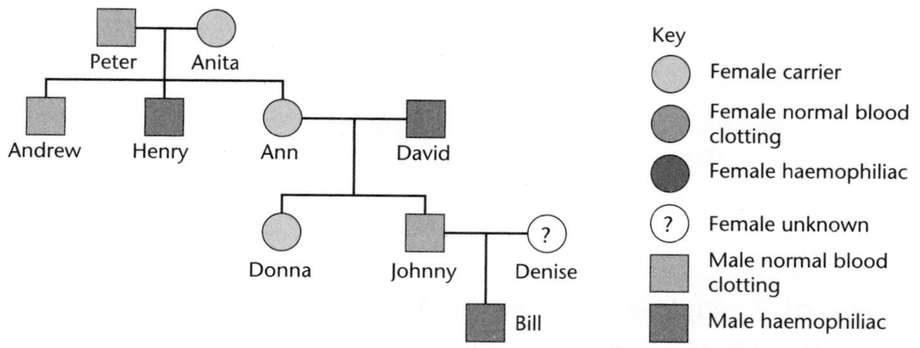

Key

⚪ Female carrier

⚪ Female normal blood clotting

⚫ Female haemophiliac

(?) Female unknown

⬜ Male normal blood clotting

⬛ Male haemophiliac

0 4 . 4 Show the **two** possible genotypes for Denise and explain how this can be deduced.

Give evidence from the genetic diagram to support your answer.

Let X^H = normal blood clotting

Let X^h = haemophiliac trait

[1 mark]

Denise's possible genotypes ....

Explanation

[2 marks]

....

....

....

....

$\boxed{0 \ 5}$ Type I diabetes is a condition, usually starting in childhood, whereby the body is unable to regulate its blood sugar levels.

$\boxed{0 \ 5} \cdot \boxed{1}$ Describe the causes and symptoms of Type I diabetes.

[4 marks]

....

....

....

....

....

....

The treatment of Type I diabetes includes the injection of insulin. A new development is a machine that acts as a continuous glucose monitor and an insulin pump. The device calculates the exact dosage of insulin required, based on the levels recorded. The insulin is then delivered automatically into the skin tissue. See **Figure 8**.

Figure 8

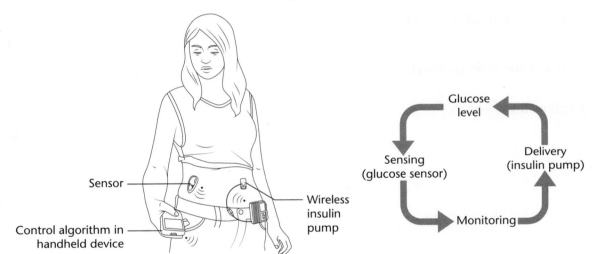

0 5 . 2 What are the advantages and disadvantages of using this method of insulin delivery instead of injections?

[4 marks]

....

....

....

....

....

....

A scientist took a blood sample from a suspected diabetic two hours after a meal and separated the plasma from the cells using centrifugation. He then made up some standard solutions of glucose. The plasma and glucose samples were then tested with Benedict's reagent. Tubes of each sample were placed in a colorimeter and the light absorbence recorded. The results for the standardised glucose samples are shown in **Figure 9**.

Figure 9

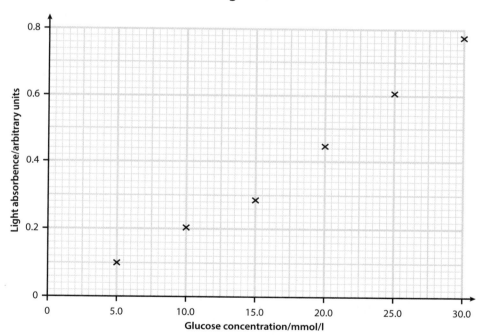

0 5 . 3 The sample from the suspected diabetic had an absorbency of 0.45 arbitrary units. Using the graph above to help you, estimate the blood glucose concentration of the suspected diabetic.

[1 mark]

....

0 5 . 4 Most adult blood glucose concentrations are below 7.0 mmol/l. What conclusions can you draw about the health of the patient? Give a reason for your answer.

[2 marks]

....

....

....

0 6 A scientist humanely trapped some mice in a small woodland. Using the mark recapture method, she estimated there were 140 wood mice altogether in the area. Some mice had a dark brown coat and others a light brown coat. Genetic studies show that the allele for dark brown (B) is dominant over the allele for light brown (b).

In the population there were 42 light brown mice.

0 6 . 1 Using the Hardy–Weinberg equations, calculate the frequency of homozygous recessive mice in the population.

[2 marks]

0 6 . 2 Using the Hardy–Weinberg equations, calculate how many heterozygotes there would be in a population of 3000 mice.

[2 marks]

0 6 . 3 Name **two** assumptions that must be made before applying the Hardy–Weinberg principle.

[2 marks]

0 7 Read the passages below.

(1) Finches from the Galapagos Islands have become one of the most popular representatives of Darwin's theory of natural selection. They embody the process of speciation forced by environmental conditions. Differences between very closely related species depend on the particular island where they originated, and the food types present there. Studies have continued on these species, and their genomes scrutinised at the molecular level in order to try to understand how exactly speciation occurs. They embody the process of allopatric speciation forced by environmental conditions.

(2) A recent study was carried out by a scientific team led by M. K. Skinner. The team compared the pattern of copy number variations (CNVs) between the genomes of different finch species. CNVs are repetitions of genetic sequences that can be related to phenotypic variation and speciation processes.

(3) Skinner also chose a particular kind of modification called DNA methylation. Methylation is an ON signal for gene activation that can be transmitted to offspring, and therefore can be an important factor in evolution. The question Skinner asked was: which kind of modifications in the finches' genomes showed a pattern that could correlate with the phenotypic differences observed in Darwin's finches? When comparing DNA or protein sequences, the study of their similarities and differences at the molecular level reflects millions of years of evolution from their common ancestors.

Based on information from http://mappingignorance.org/2014/12/01/epigenetics-takes-us-back-galapagos/

0 7 . 1 The term **allopatric speciation** is used in paragraph 1. Explain the difference between allopatric and sympatric speciation.

In each instance use an example other than Darwin's finches to illustrate your answer.

[4 marks]

0 7 . 2 The terms **genetic sequences** and **genome** are used in the texts. Both involve studying the molecule DNA. How would the data produced from these two types of study differ?

[2 marks]

....

....

....

0 7 . 3 Suggest how CNVs (paragraph 2) might be used to identify common ancestors and the pattern of speciation.

[2 marks]

....

....

0 7 . 4 What property of the methylation process makes it useful for studying evolution?

[2 marks]

....

....

The diagram (**Figure 10**) shows a possible evolutionary tree for several species of Galapagos finches.

Figure 10

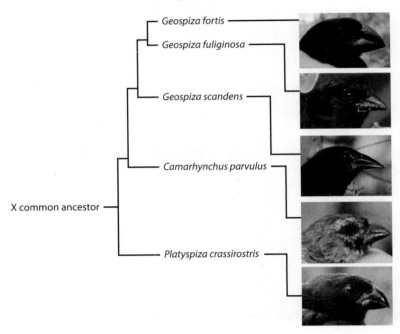

X common ancestor

A finch's beak is adapted to the type of food it eats. A larger beak is better for consuming larger nuts, whereas a smaller, thinner beak is more advantageous for dealing with smaller seeds.

0 7 · 5 Species X is termed a common ancestor. Use Darwin's theory of natural selection along with what you know about speciation to explain how the common ancestor could have given rise to the five species shown.

[5 marks]

....

....

....

....

....

....

....

....

0 8 Genes can be inserted into crop plants to produce varieties better suited to meet the demands of food supply. For example, Golden Rice contains a gene that produces vitamin A. Lack of vitamin A in the diet can lead to a condition called xerophthalmia. The bacterial vector used to insert the coding gene is *Agrobacterium tumefaciens,* a plant pathogen that causes tumour-like swellings, called galls, to grow.

Figure 11 shows the biotechnological process used to produce a transgenic plant.

Figure 11

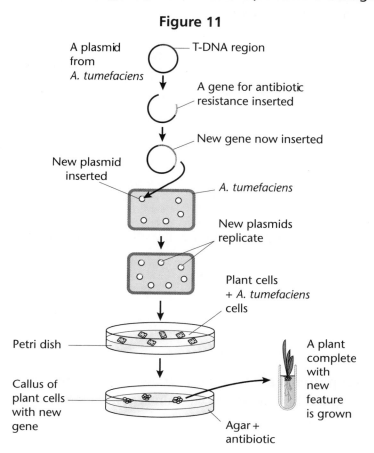

0 8 . 1 In stage 1 of this procedure, a section of the pathogenic bacterial DNA (the T-DNA region) is removed. The discarded code produces proteins that interfere in a plant's production of cytokinins and auxins. Suggest how the removal of this DNA prevents pathogenic action of the bacterium.

[1 mark]

....

....

0 8 · **2** What type of enzymes are used to remove genes in this way?

[1 mark]

_____

0 8 · **3** Explain how the insertion of a gene coding for antibiotic resistance ensures that only plants containing vitamin A are produced.

[2 marks]

_____

_____

_____

_____

0 8 · **4** The plant cells used in stage 2 have their cell walls removed. Why is this necessary?

[1 mark]

_____

_____

0 8 · **5** A symptom of xerophthalmia is 'night blindness.' A pigment called rhodopsin is derived from vitamin A. Explain how a lack of vitamin A could lead to night blindness.

[2 marks]

_____

_____

Figure 12 shows the structure of a rod cell taken from a human retina.

Figure 12

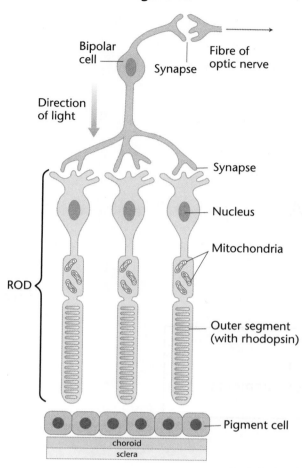

Use the diagram to explain how bright light causes the rod cell to initiate an action potential in an axon from the optic nerve.

[5 marks]

....

....

....

....

....

....

....

END OF QUESTIONS

A-level
Biology
Practice paper for AQA

Paper 3

Time allowed: 2 hours

Materials
For this paper you must have:
- a ruler with millimetre measurements
- a calculator.

Instructions
- Use black ink or black ball-point pen.
- Fill in the boxes at the bottom of this page.
- Answer **all** questions in Section **A**.
- Answer **one** question from Section **B**.

Information
- The marks for questions are shown in brackets.
- The maximum mark for this paper is 78.

Name: ....

Section A

Answer **all** questions in this section.

0 1   **Figure 1** shows a simplified biochemical pathway for glycolysis and the link reaction in mammals.

Figure 1

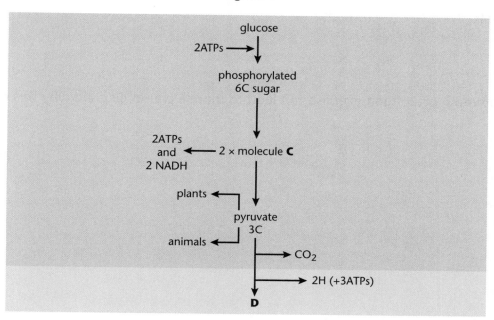

0 1 . 1 Name molecules **C** and **D**.

[1 mark]

....

....

0 1 . 2 In aerobic respiration, reduced coenzyme produced in glycolysis (NADH) is reduced later in the mitochondria and recycled as NAD once more. Explain why glycolysis would stop if the NADH was not used in this way.

[1 mark]

....

....

....

0 1 . 3 During anaerobic respiration, NADH is recycled in a different manner. Describe the fate of NADH in plants and animals undergoing anaerobic respiration.

[1 mark]

Plants ....

[1 mark]

Animals ....

....

0 1 . 4 In mammals, prolonged exercise can lead to muscle cramp. Explain why this occurs.

[2 marks]

....

....

....

0 2 Insulin is a polypeptide hormone produced in pancreatic tissue. Below is part of the DNA base sequence found in the gene for the polypeptide:

GCA   TAT   AGA   CCA   TCT   GAA   ACA   CTG   TGC   GGC

Figure 2 shows a matrix that can be used to identify the particular amino acid coded for by a triplet of bases in the DNA template.

Figure 2

Second organic base

First organic base	A	G	T	C	Third organic base
A	AAA ⎤ Phe AAG ⎦ AAT ⎤ Leu AAC ⎦	AGA ⎤ AGG ⎥ Ser AGT ⎥ AGC ⎦	ATA ⎤ Tyr ATG ⎦ ATT Stop ATC Stop	ACA ⎤ Cys ACG ⎦ ACT Stop ACC Trp	A G T C
G	GAA ⎤ GAG ⎥ Leu GAT ⎥ GAC ⎦	GGA ⎤ GGG ⎥ Pro GGT ⎥ GGC ⎦	GTA ⎤ His GTG ⎦ GTT ⎤ Gln GTC ⎦	GCA ⎤ GCG ⎥ Arg GCT ⎥ GCC ⎦	A G T C
T	TAA ⎤ TAG ⎥ Ile TAT ⎦ TAC Met	TGA ⎤ TGG ⎥ Thr TGT ⎥ TGC ⎦	TTA ⎤ Asn TTG ⎦ TTT ⎤ Lys TTC ⎦	TCA ⎤ Ser TCG ⎦ TCT ⎤ Arg TCC ⎦	A G T C
C	CAA ⎤ CAG ⎥ Val CAT ⎥ CAC ⎦	CGA ⎤ CGG ⎥ Ala CGT ⎥ CGC ⎦	CTA ⎤ Asp CTG ⎦ CTT ⎤ Glu CTC ⎦	CCA ⎤ CCG ⎥ Gly CCT ⎥ CCC ⎦	A G T C

0 2 . 1 Use the information to deduce the amino acid sequence for this section of the polypeptide. The first amino acid has been identified for you.

[1 mark]

Arg   ____   ____   ____   ____   ____   ____   ____   ____   ____

0 2 . 2 DNA is replicated during the cell cycle prior to a mitotic division. Describe the events that occur in DNA replication. State the names of any other enzymes involved.

1 The DNA begins to unwind under the influence of the enzyme DNA helicase.

2 .... **[1 mark]**

....

3 .... **[1 mark]**

....

4 .... **[1 mark]**

....

Cells that undergo mitosis are usually controlled by external signals. Oestrogen is a growth factor and acts as a regulator for cell division. Sometimes, human breast tissue cells arise that do not possess oestrogen receptors.

Cancer cells do not show **contact inhibition**. This is where cells stop dividing due to signals sent from neighbouring cells.

0 2 . 3 Using this information, explain how a cell without oestrogen receptors can become a cancerous tumour.

[3 marks]

Genetic sequencing experiments have led to treatments for **melanoma**, a form of skin cancer. A new **kinase inhibitor** drug targets the gene that signals the growth of new blood cells in melanoma tumours.

Figure 3 shows how the blood cells are normally manufactured.

Figure 3

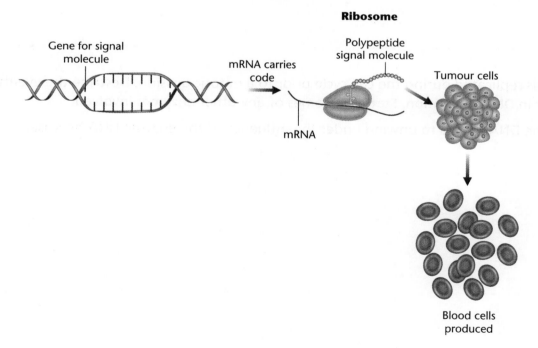

0 2 . 4 Using this information, and your knowledge of protein synthesis, explain how the drug can stop the growth of cancerous tumours.

[4 marks]

....

....

....

....

....

Figure 4 shows how the release of a neurotransmitter called serotonin occurs at a synapse. Drugs called selective serotonin re-uptake inhibitors (or SSRIs) are used in the treatment of depression. Serotonin binds to receptor sites on the post-synaptic membrane and triggers the transmission of impulses. These impulses stimulate areas of the brain associated with the cardiovascular system, muscles, and mood. SSRIs act on serotonin transport molecules on the pre-synaptic membrane.

Figure 4

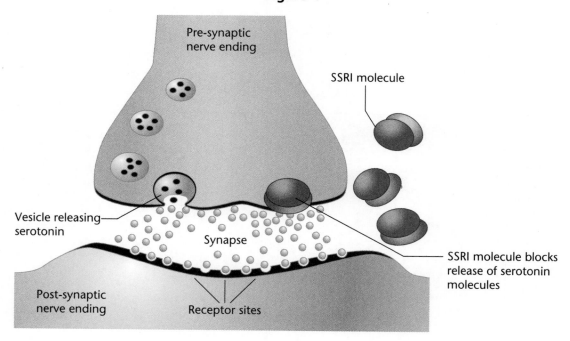

0 3 · 1 Explain how SSRI molecules are able to reduce symptoms of depression.

[4 marks]

_____

_____

_____

_____

_____

_____

_____

_____

Parkinson's disease occurs commonly in the elderly. It results from the degeneration of neurones that produce dopamine. Dopamine is a neurotransmitter that binds to specialised dopamine receptors on the post-synaptic membrane. This binding triggers the generation of action potentials, resulting in lifted mood or even euphoria, depending on the amount of dopamine present. It is also involved in the control of muscle contraction.

0 3 . 2 One type of drug contains a molecule precursor of dopamine. Suggest how this drug would benefit a patient suffering from Parkinson's disease.

[2 marks]

....

....

....

0 3 . 3 Methylenedioxymethamphetamine is a drug that stimulates vesicles in dopamine-releasing neurones and also blocks re-uptake transporter molecules on the pre-synaptic membrane. Explain on a **molecular** level how MDMA produces feelings of well-being.

[2 marks]

....

....

....

....

0 3 . 4 Explain the importance of summation at a synapse.

[2 marks]

....

....

....

....

0 4   **Figure 5** shows the structure of an antibody in the class known as **immunoglobulin** G or IgG

Figure 5

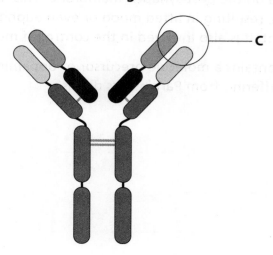

C

0 4 . 1 Name the site on the antibody labelled **C**.

[1 mark

_____

0 4 . 2 Describe how the site labelled **C** is involved in defending the body against invading pathogens.

[2 marks

_____

_____

_____

Viperids are a family of snakes that produce venom containing polypeptide toxins. The polypeptide is often an enzyme that coagulates blood – a haemotoxin. When a victim is bitten, it is sometimes difficult to identify the species of snake responsible and therefore administering the correct anti-venom can be problematic.

Scientists have developed a technique for developing polyvalent anti-venoms. These are effective against a range of snake venoms.

Figure 6 shows how snake venom can be identified.

Figure 6

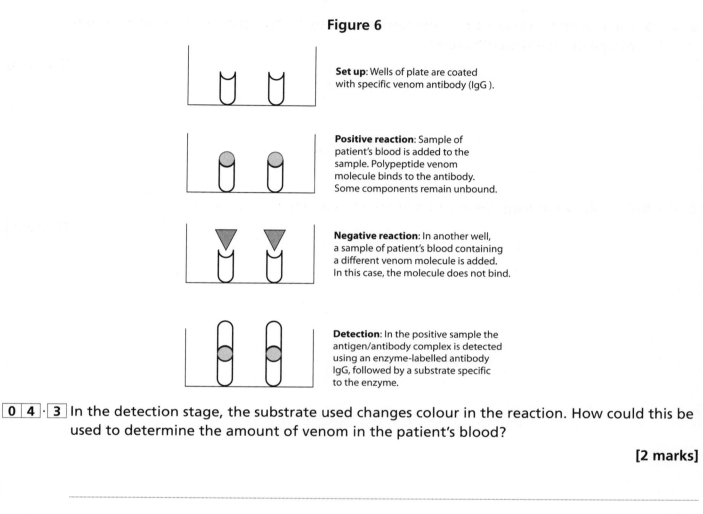

Set up: Wells of plate are coated with specific venom antibody (IgG).

Positive reaction: Sample of patient's blood is added to the sample. Polypeptide venom molecule binds to the antibody. Some components remain unbound.

Negative reaction: In another well, a sample of patient's blood containing a different venom molecule is added. In this case, the molecule does not bind.

Detection: In the positive sample the antigen/antibody complex is detected using an enzyme-labelled antibody IgG, followed by a substrate specific to the enzyme.

0 4 . 3   In the detection stage, the substrate used changes colour in the reaction. How could this be used to determine the amount of venom in the patient's blood?

[2 marks]

....

....

0 4 · 4 Explain how this technique could be used to develop a **polyvalent anti-venom**.

[2 marks]

_____

_____

0 4 · 5 Using what you know about the tertiary structure of proteins, suggest how venom coagulates the patient's blood.

[2 marks]

_____

_____

_____

0 4 · 6 Describe what happens in a phagocyte after a pathogen is engulfed.

[2 marks]

_____

_____

_____

Plastic debris has been accumulating in marine habitats for decades, to the extent that estimated annual build-up measures in millions of tonnes. Large, persistent congregations of plastic items are quite visible. What isn't as obvious, is the hidden build-up of microscopic fragments and fibres, together with microbeads, a commonly used component in exfoliating products such as toothpastes. See **Figure 7** and **Figure 8**.

Figure 7

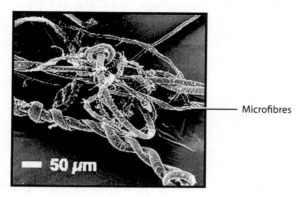

Microfibres

Figure 8

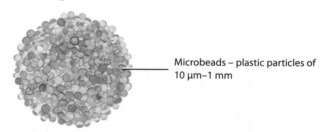

Microbeads – plastic particles of 10 μm–1 mm

To quantify the abundance of microplastics, scientists carried out an investigation.

Sediments were collected from 18 beaches and from their associated estuarine and sub-tidal sediments.

Particles were separated by flotation to remove natural particulate material.

The findings are shown in **Figure 9**.

Figure 9

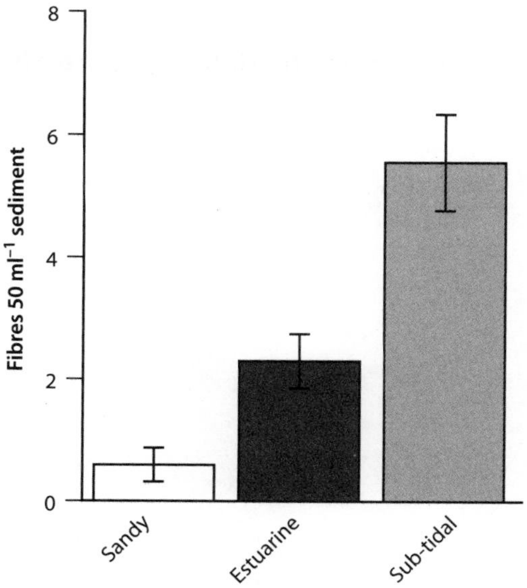

0 5 · 1 What property of the sediment particles is utilised by the separation procedure?

[1 mark]

....

0 5 · 2 What conclusions can be drawn from the data in **Figure 9**?

[2 marks]

....

....

....

To assess long-term trends in abundance, data from plankton samples collected since the 1960s were analysed. The findings are shown in **Figure 10**.

Figure 10

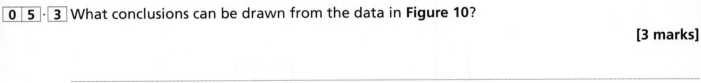

0 5 · 3 What conclusions can be drawn from the data in **Figure 10**?

[3 marks]

....

....

....

....

To determine the potential for microscopic plastics to be ingested, the scientists kept amphipods (detritivores), lugworms (deposit feeders), and barnacles (filter feeders) in aquaria with small quantities of microscopic plastics. All three species ingested plastics within a few days.

0 5 . 4 Suggest why the scientists used these organisms for their experiment.

[2 marks]

....

....

....

0 5 . 5 In their paper, the scientists said '. . . it remains to be shown whether toxic substances can pass from plastics to the food chain.' Using information from **Figure 9** and **Figure 10**, comment on their statement.

[2 marks]

....

....

....

Another study of plastics pollution looked at how vertebrates were affected by microbeads. It showed that plastic polymers are 'sponges' for toxins such as DDT and chemicals called PCBs. Microbeads were found to accumulate up to one million times the concentration of these toxins compared to the concentration floating in the water itself.

0 5 . 6 Explain why high concentrations of these toxins might affect vertebrates more than the invertebrates found lower in the food chain.

[2 marks]

....

....

....

Table 1 shows the concentrations of three types of PCB found in different organs of the fish *O. mossambicus*.

Table 1

PCB levels in *O. mossambicus* tissues ($n = 9$, $ng \cdot g^{-1}$, mean ± standard deviation)				
Analytes	Muscle (*n*=9)	Gills (*n*=9)	Gonads (*n*=9)	Liver (*n*=9)
PCB 28	6.47 ± 6.94	7.89 ± 5.48	9.45 ± 10.60	15.26 ± 6.57
PCB 52	3.42 ± 2.33	7.97 ± 4.93	7.97 ± 4.66	17.73 ± 6.34
PCB 101	6.38 ± 4.54	8.34 ± 6.77	8.50 ± 5.49	16.90 ± 3.13

0 5 . 7   A student looked at the data and concluded that PCBs accumulate more in fish livers than in any other organ. Explain why this conclusion may be unreliable.

[3 marks]

_____

_____

_____

_____

_____

Section B

Answer **one** question.

0 6   Write an essay on **one** of the topics below.

EITHER

0 6 · 1 The effects of global warming on the distribution and internal processes of organisms.

[25 marks]

OR

0 6 · 2 The mechanisms by which substances are transported within cells and across the cell surface membrane.

[25 marks]

END OF QUESTIONS

Answers

Note: Words within answers that appear in **bold** must be used/spelled correctly.

Paper 1

0 1 . 1 α–helix [1 mark, both needed to gain mark]

0 1 . 2 Water [1 mark]

0 1 . 3 Ring drawn around either central H atom on glycine [1 mark]

0 1 . 4 **Any two from**:

$$O \quad H \quad H$$
$$\| \quad | \quad |$$
$$-C - N - C-$$
$$\quad \quad \quad |$$
$$\quad \quad \quad H$$

bond shown between C and N; OH and H removed; = O and –H remain. [2 marks]

0 1 . 5 **Any two from**: individual polypeptide chains are held in place/fixed; by hydrogen bonds between molecules; by cross-linkages between amino acid R-groups; in adjacent chains; reference to quaternary structure of triple helix. [2 marks: 1 mark for each explanation]

0 2 . 1 Denaturation [1 mark]

0 2 . 2 **Any three from**: heat causes bonds (e.g. hydrogen bonds/disulphide bridges) to break; polypeptide chains unfold; then become tangled together; causes precipitation/polypeptides no longer soluble. [3 marks: 1 mark for each explanation]

0 2 . 3 Add dilute sodium hydroxide and dilute copper sulfate/biuret solution to the sample [1 mark]; A violet/purple colour appears if a protein is present [1 mark].

0 2 . 4 Endopeptidases break peptide links/bonds between amino acids **in the middle** of polypeptide chains [1 mark]; Exopeptidases break the peptide links of the amino acids at the **ends** of the chains [1 mark]; Exopeptidases form shorter polypeptides/dipeptides [1 mark].

0 3 . 1 25 mmol^{-1} [1 mark]

0 3 . 2 Temperature: **Thermostatically controlled** water bath/or described [1 mark].

pH: Buffer solution **set at optimum/ appropriate pH value** (range) [1 mark].

0 3 . 3 **Any two from**: enzyme converts sucrose/breaks it down; products/glucose and fructose do not crystallise/remain liquefied; increases time taken for food to spoil. [2 marks: 1 mark for each explanation]

0 3 . 4 Domain: Eukaryota
Phylum: Ascomycota
Genus: Saccharomycetales.
[2 marks for all three correct, 1 mark for two correct, 0 mark for 0 or one correct]

0 4 . 1 Name of structure A is the nucleus.

Function of structure A is to store genetic material/DNA/chromatin; controls the cell's activities [requires correct name and one function to gain 1 mark].

0 4 . 2 Lysosomes contain digestive enzymes [1 mark]; Macrophage uses enzymes to digest/break down material it has ingested/engulfed [1 mark].

0 4 . 3 Actual diameter of X = size of image/ magnification = 4/6000 = 0.00067 cm = 6.67 μm. [2 marks for correct answer in micrometres, 1 mark if answer is 0.00067 or working shown as 4/6000]

0 5 . 1 Stains – (acetic) orcein or toluidine blue

Any four from: cut small length of the root tips; put tips in a small volume of ethanoic acid (on a watchglass); for 10 minutes; wash the root tips then dry on filter paper; heat hydrochloric acid (to 60 °C) in a water bath; transfer the root tips to the hot hydrochloric acid (and leave for 5 minutes); wash the root tips again in cold water and dry on filter paper; (use mounted needle to) remove some root tips onto a **clean** microscope slide; cut each about 2 mm from the growing root tip (discard the rest); add a small drop of stain (and leave for 2 minutes); break up the tissue with a mounted needle/seeker; cover with a coverslip and squash/description of squash. [5 marks: 1 mark for stain, 4 marks for each description]

0 5 . 2 14 mitotic cells, but allow any answer between 10–25 [no mark for this]. Therefore any value between 7%–19% [2 marks, answer must be consistent with student's own count].

06·1 Regular cell shape with cell wall, cytoplasm and central vacuole shown **[1 mark]**; Cytoplasm pulled away from cell wall in at least one place/completely detached from cell wall – cytoplasm must be labelled **[1 mark]**.

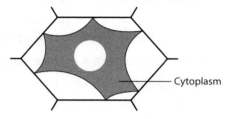
Cytoplasm

06·2 **Any two from**: external solution/soil water has a **lower** water potential; water will leave by **osmosis**; plasmolysis would lead to wilting/plant not able to absorb water for its life processes. **[2 marks: 1 mark for each explanation]**

06·3 Red pigment allows cell contents/cytoplasm/protoplast to be seen more clearly **[1 mark]**.

06·4 10.4% **[1 mark]**

06·5 Correct **linear** scale taking up more than half of the grid area **[1 mark]**; Correct plotting **[1 mark]**; Smooth curve/straight line through points **[1 mark, no mark for bar graph]**.

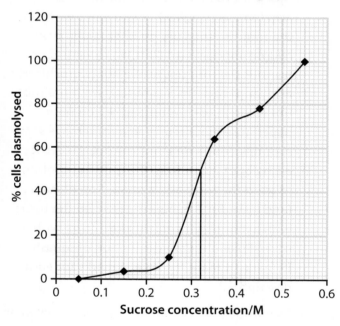

06·6 Two correct lines drawn at 50% plasmolysis **[1 mark]**; Correct molarity of onion cells – 0.32 M **[1 mark, error within plus or minus 0.02 M will be allowed]**.

07·1 (Logarithmic scale) needed so that all data can be seen in the space available/difference between elephant and shrew is so great that the data would not fit on a linear scale **[1 mark]**.

07·2 **At least one from**: as body mass increases, metabolic rate per gram per hour decreases; for body masses greater than 1.05 kg, the differences between metabolic rates are less pronounced.

At least one from: smaller animals have a greater surface area for their mass than larger ones; therefore, they lose heat at a faster rate; and require more energy to maintain a constant core temperature; smaller animals, e.g. shrews, are more active as they need to eat a proportionately higher mass of food each day. **[3 marks: 1 mark for each explanation]**

07·3 **Any two from**: protists have a large surface area to volume ratio, or reverse argument (ORA); shorter diffusion pathway to all parts of organism (ORA); diffusion an adequate method for exchanging gases in protists/larger organisms require specialised organs to transport respiratory gases long distances. **[2 marks: 1 mark for each explanation]**

08·1 0.3 seconds **[1 mark]**

08·2 **10.2** Must be marked between 0.5 and 0.7 seconds **[1 mark]**.

08·3 The atrium has a higher pressure than the ventricle to ensure blood flows into the ventricle **[1 mark]**.

08·4 **Any two from**: atrioventricular valves are closed; to prevent backflow of blood; into atria. **[2 marks: 1 mark for each explanation]**

08·5 0.11 litres per minute **[2 marks, but if incorrect answer 7.15 divided by 65 gains 1 mark]**.

08·6 **Any three from**: blood is transported more quickly; more oxygen taken up at the lungs/more carbon dioxide excreted at the lungs; more oxygen reaches the muscles; more glucose reaches the muscles; so muscles contract more effectively. **[3 marks: 1 mark for each explanation]**

09·1 **Any two from**: haemoglobin has a high affinity (attraction) for oxygen (at this partial pressure); it becomes highly saturated with oxygen; sigmoid or 'S'-shaped dissociation curve/properties of haemoglobin mean that a small change in partial pressure causes a massive loading of oxygen. **[2 marks: 1 mark for each explanation]**

09·**2** **Any two from**: the dissociation curve is moved to the right/Bohr shift; more oxygen is 'off-loaded' to the muscle; carbon dioxide lowers the affinity of the haemoglobin for oxygen. **[2 marks: 1 mark for each explanation]**

09·**3** The curve should be drawn **above the** normal line with the **same** origin **[1 mark]**.

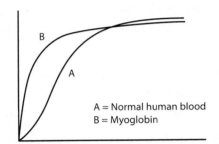

A = Normal human blood
B = Myoglobin

09·**4** Myoglobin remains bound to oxygen when whale is submerged **[1 mark]**; Oxygen store in muscle can be used to supply the needs of respiration while under water **[1 mark]**.

10·**1** Plot A species diversity = 3.94 **[1 mark]**;
Plot B species diversity = 2.70 **[1 mark]**

Working as follows:

Plot A: N = 46, total n(n − 1) = 526, therefore (46 × 45)/526 = 3.94

Plot B: N = 42, total n(n − 1) = 638, therefore (42 × 41)/638 = 2.70

10·**2** **Plot A has a greater diversity** as it has been left uncultivated longer than Plot B **[1 mark]**; Greater opportunity for new species to colonise in Plot A/species have more time to multiply in number or reproduce/habitat has more time to recover from effects of cultivation or eradication of wild species **[1 mark]**.

10·**3** For Rosebay willow herb, the difference in number is probably due to chance/probability – the likelihood of this is more than 5%/0.05 **[1 mark]**; For all the other species, the difference in number is unlikely to be due to chance **[1 mark]**; Because P for these species < 0.05, which is significant/is lower than 5%/0.05 **[1 mark]**.

11 **Any two from**: ATP is formed from a molecule of ribose and adenine; and three phosphate groups; **[these 2 marks can be gained from a suitable molecular diagram]**; ATP is synthesised by the **condensation** of ADP and Pi; catalysed by the enzyme **ATP synthase**.

Any three from: ATP can release its energy as a small 'packet' by **hydrolysis**; controlled by the enzyme **ATP hydrolase**; inorganic phosphate released; can be coupled to energy-requiring reactions within cells/suitable example, e.g. synthesis of large molecules, active transport; ATP can be used to phosphorylate other compounds, often making them more reactive/reference to photosynthesis or respiration. **[5 marks: 1 mark for each explanation]**

12 **At least one from**: transpiration occurs in **xylem** (dead cells); transpiration flow carries **water** and **mineral ions**; movement of water in transpiration due to combination of **root pressure** and **cohesion-tension**; reference to **capillarity** contributing to **cohesion** (water molecules have an attraction for each other so when one water molecule moves others move with it); water molecules are attracted to the sides of the vessels, which pulls the water upwards (adhesion); transpiration causes a very negative water potential in the mesophyll of the leaves/water in the xylem is of higher water potential.

At least one from: translocation occurs in **phloem**; translocation occurs via mass flow/cytoplasmic streaming; translocation involves transport of carbohydrate/sucrose and amino acids; reference to companion cells/possession of cytoplasm and mitochondria/cells are living. **[6 marks: 1 mark for each explanation]**

13 **At least one from**: vaccines consist of attenuated pathogens/non-harmful antigens; antigens trigger B-lymphocytes/humoral immune system to produce antibodies; they stimulate the production of memory cells; so that the person develops **active artificial immunity**.

At least one from: **herd immunity** – explanation of herd immunity, e.g. the vaccination of a significant proportion of a population (or herd) makes it difficult for a disease to spread; because there are so few susceptible people left to infect. **[4 marks: 1 mark for each explanation]**

Paper 2

01.1 To release carbon dioxide for fixation in light-independent reaction/photosynthesis **[1 mark]**.

01.2 To ensure light-dependent reactions had stopped/to analyse compounds formed at a particular time **[1 mark, 'to stop photosynthesis/kill algae' insufficient]**.

01.3 To release compounds from cells/to break up cells/to enable compounds to be identified **[1 mark]**.

01.4 A: glycerate 3-phosphate (first compound to be formed in light-independent reaction and therefore first to contain radioactive carbon) **[1 mark]**.

B: triose phosphate (formed later, hence not seen on 5-second chromatogram) **[1 mark]**.

01.5 54.6% **[2 marks]** but $(6.8 - 4.4)/4.4 \times 100$ **[1 mark]**

01.6 Existing ribulose bisphosphate forms glycerate 3-phosphate, which increases **[1 mark]**; No reduced NADP or ATP to continue reaction (supplied from light-dependent phase), therefore levels out **[1 mark]**.

01.7 No triose phosphate formed as no reduced NADP or ATP available **[1 mark]**; therefore no compound starting point available for formation of more ribulose bisphosphate **[1 mark]**.

01.8 Two carbon rings circled, as shown below **[1 mark]**.

Ribulose bisphosphate

01.9 Rubisco/RuBP carboxylase/ribulose bisphosphate carboxylase **[1 mark]**.

02.1 Nitrification **[1 mark]**

02.2 Atmospheric nitrogen converted to ammonium **[1 mark, 'ammonia' will not be accepted]**; Nitrogen in ammonium needed for amino acids/protein/nucleic acids **[1 mark]**.

02.3 **Any two from:** water fills air spaces/causes lower oxygen content; anaerobic conditions encourage growth of **denitrifying bacteria**; nitrate converted back to molecular/atmospheric nitrogen. **[2 marks: 1 mark for each explanation]**

02.4 Insects trapped/digested are a source of protein **[1 mark]**; Protein is broken down in body of plant to release nitrogen/nitrate **[1 mark]**.

02.5 To incorporate into/build ATP molecule/build DNA to prevent poor growth/poor quality fruit/blue or green leaves **[1 mark]**.

02.6 $r = 0.84$ **[3 marks for correct answer, but correct numerator – 243 910 – will gain 1 mark, and correct denominator – 289 204, i.e. 243 910/289 204 – will gain 1 mark]**

02.7 'Yes' – 0.84/answer to 'Explanation' is a significant correlation **or** if r is miscalculated at <0.5. 'No', r is not a significant correlation, will be allowed.

However, data may not be valid due to small sample size/timing of sample/phosphate may have entered waterway at different points/algae may not have had time to respond/other mineral nutrients not accounted for, etc. **[1 mark: No mark for 'Yes' or 'No', must be justfied.]**

02.8 **Any three from:** growth of algal blooms on surface; blocks off sunlight; less photosynthesis; plants/algae die; aerobic bacteria break down dead plant material; oxygen absorbed from water; animals, e.g. fish, die **due to lack of oxygen ['algae kill animals' will not be allowed]**. **[3 marks: 1 mark for each description]**

03.1 There is no significant difference between the number of woodlice found in dark and light/woodlice have no preference for light or dark conditions **[1 mark]**.

03.2 **Any two from:** woodlice of the same age/size; constant room temperature; constant humidity; uniform/lack of vibration/noise; controlled/no handling of woodlice/use of brush or similar to avoid trauma; removal of olfactory/chemical secretions from woodlice (by using fresh choice chamber/base) when performing replicates. **[2 marks: 1 mark for each variable]**

03.3

	Light	Dark
Observed results (O)	39	61
Expected results (E)	50	50
$(O-E)^2$	121	121
$(O-E)^2/E$	2.42	2.42

Correct value of χ^2 is 4.84 **[1 mark for correct value of χ^2; 1 mark for correct totals in raw data table; 1 mark for correct completion of chi-squared table]**

03.4 If χ^2 correct, then 4.84 is greater than critical value **[1 mark]**; Therefore null hypothesis is rejected/probability that difference in distribution is due to chance is <0.05/5% **[1 mark]**.

03.5 Directional response **[1 mark]**; Away from (touch) stimulus **[1 mark]**.

04.1

RrYy   ×   RrYy

gametes   (RY) (Ry) (rY) (ry)   (RY) (Ry) (rY) (ry)

[1 mark, all must be correct, can be in any order]

	RY	Ry	rY	ry
RY	RRYY	RRYy	RrYY	RrYy
Ry	RRYy	RRyy	RrYy	Rryy
rY	RrYY	RrYy	rrYY	rrYy
ry	RrYy	Rryy	rrYy	rryy

[2 marks for completely correct table, every incorrect genotype subtracts 1 mark]

04.2 9 round and yellow:3 green and round: 3 yellow and round:1 yellow and wrinkly **[1 mark, all must be correct]**

04.3 **Any two from**: linkage between chromosomes; numbers in sample not high enough to show expected ratios; loci of genes may be close together on the same chromosome. **[2 marks: 1 mark for each reason]**

04.4 Denise's possible genotypes: X^HX^h or X^hX^h **[1 mark]**

Explanation: Johnny is X^HY, so he is responsible for Bill's Y chromosome (Y chromosomes do not carry a blood clotting gene) **[1 mark]**; Working backwards, Bill is haemophiliac so Denise must have at least one X^h **[1 mark]**.

05.1 **Any three from**: the pancreas fails to produce enough insulin; after a meal when blood glucose concentrations increase, the level remains high; high blood glucose causes hyperglycaemia; kidneys cannot reabsorb glucose, causing glucose presence in urine. **[3 marks: 1 mark for each description]**

One symptom from: dehydration; loss of weight; increased risk of infection; genital itching; lethargy. **[1 mark]**

05.2 Advantages, **any two from**: better/more precisely controlled blood glucose levels/less likely to become hyper- or hypo-glycaemic; the system simulates the body more precisely; no need to manually check glucose levels by blood testing; improved quality of life. Disadvantages, **any two from**: more expensive/ may not be available for everybody on the NHS; possible malfunctions in control unit could lead to incorrect insulin dosages; closed-loop system – cannot use manual injections as a back-up if problems occur. **[4 marks: 1 mark for each advantage, 1 mark for each disadvantage]**

05.3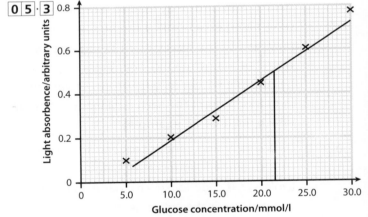

Straight line (of best fit) to be drawn on graph, 21.5 mmol/l **[1 mark, error of plus or minus 0.5 will be accepted if answer incorrect]**

05.4 Patient has blood glucose levels significantly higher than that of a normal/average/healthy adult **[1 mark]**; Therefore, the patient is likely to have diabetes **[1 mark]**.

06.1 From $p^2 + 2pq + q^2 = 1$ then number of homozygous recessive mice (light brown) = $q^2 = 42/140 = 0.3$ or 30% **[2 marks for correct answer, if answer is incorrect, then 1 mark awarded for correct application of this Hardy–Weinberg equation]**

0 6 . 2 $q = \sqrt{0.3} = 0.55$, then from $p + q = 1$, $p = 1 - 0.55 = 0.45$, then Heterozygote frequency = $2pq = 2 \times 0.45 \times 0.55 = 0.5$. In a population of 3000, this would be 1500 heterozygote mice **[2 marks for correct answer, if answer is incorrect, then 1 mark is given for correct application of this Hardy–Weinberg equation (up to $2 \times 0.45 \times 0.55$)]**.

0 6 . 3 **Any two from:** there must be no immigration or emigration; no mutations; no selection (natural or artificial); must be true random mating; all genotypes must be equally fertile. **[2 marks: 1 mark for each assumption]**

0 7 . 1 **Any four from:**

Allopatric speciation takes place after geographical isolation; Named example, e.g. the rising of sea level splits a population of animals formerly connected by land to create two islands; Mutations take place so that two groups result in different species.

Sympatric speciation takes place through genetic variation; In the same geographical area; Mutation may result in reproductive incompatibility; Named example, e.g. a structure in birds may lead to a different song being produced by the new variant; This may lead to the new variant being rejected from the mainstream group; Breeding may be possible within its own group of variants **[4 marks: 1 mark for each explanation, one of which must be an example]**.

0 7 . 2 Data concerning genetic sequencing would contain limited sequences of bases/codons/triplets that code for specific genes **[1 mark]**; The genome is the entire genetic code of an organism, therefore will contain the sequences that code for thousands of genes **[1 mark]**.

0 7 . 3 **Any two from:** more closely related species will share a greater proportion of CNVs; common ancestor(s) will share CNVs with more than one line of descendents; evidence from these studies can be used to reinforce observations from other phenotypic variations and, thus, establish evolutionary trees. **[2 marks: 1 mark for each suggestion]**

0 7 . 4 **Any two from:** presence of certain methyl groups determine which genes are switched on; increased methylation reduces transcription of genes; therefore common phenotypic traits can be used to assess how closely certain species are related; presence of certain proteins (and their switched-on genes) gives information about common ancestry. **[2 marks: 1 mark for each property]**

0 7 . 5 **Any five from:**

Natural selection: beak size/shape/type coded for by particular alleles/genes; range of alleles/genes produces range of beak types within a population; conditions/food availability in different habitats/islands acts as a **selective pressure**; the better adapted variants within the common ancestral population survive, e.g. greater amount of larger nuts favours a larger beak; these individuals are more likely to reproduce and pass on these **alleles** (NOT genes) to the next generation; allele for advantageous trait becomes more common in a population.

Speciation: emergence of new species takes place when isolation (geographic or reproductive) occurs, e.g. separation by ocean flooding (production of islands); over time separated populations can no longer interbreed. **[5 marks: 1 mark for each explanation]**

0 8 . 1 Bacteria can no longer interfere with growth (caused by cytokinins and auxins), therefore no tumours are formed **[1 mark]**.

0 8 . 2 Restriction endonucleases **[1 mark]**

0 8 . 3 Antibiotic kills those bacterial cells that have not taken up the resistance DNA coding **[1 mark]**; Hence, plant cells can only be infected with bacteria that have taken up the desired gene for vitamin A **[1 mark]**.

0 8 . 4 To allow bacterial plasmids to be taken up by the plant cell **[1 mark]**

0 8 . 5 No retinol available for pigment in **rods** **[1 mark]**; Rod cells are responsible for night vision **[1 mark]**.

0 8 . 6 Light falls on photosynthetic pigments in rod **[1 mark]**; Chemical change in receptor – rhodopsin $\rightarrow$ opsin + retinal **[1 mark]**; Opsin opens ion channels in the cell surface membrane **[1 mark]**; Causing influx of sodium ions **[1 mark]**; Depolarisation of axon initiates action/generator potential **[1 mark]**.

Paper 3

01·1 C: glycerate 3-phosphate/G3P; D: acetyl co-enzyme A **[1 mark for both correct]**

01·2 NADH needs to be oxidised/hydrogen taken away so that it can continue to accept hydrogen in glycolysis **[1 mark]**.

01·3 Plants: (hydrogen accepted by) pyruvate (and) converted to ethanol **[1 mark]**.

Animals: (hydrogen accepted by) pyruvate (and) converted to lactate **[1 mark]**.

01·4 Build up of lactate **[1 mark]**; Lactate is a poison/toxic/damages muscle tissue, causes muscle cramp **[1 mark]**.

02·1 Arg **Ile Ser Gly Arg Leu Cys Asp Thr Pro** **[all correct for 1 mark]**

02·2 2 **Hydrogen bonds** between the two chains **break** and the two strands separate **[1 mark]**.

3 Each **complementary strand** then acts as a **template** to build its opposite strand **from free nucleotides [1 mark]**.

4 The enzyme **DNA polymerase joins the nucleotides together** (this process results in the production of two identical copies of double-stranded DNA) **[1 mark]**.

02·3 **Any three from**: breast tissue cells without receptors no longer require oestrogen to trigger mitosis/cell division; **mitosis** occurs spontaneously/is not controlled/not stopped; signals from neighbouring cells ineffective/cancer cells do not respond to neighbouring cells' signals; cancer cells divide to produce large mass/tumour. **[3 marks: 1 mark for each explanation]**

02·4 **Any four from**: drug/inhibitor prevents transcription of signal molecule gene; signal molecule/polypeptide no longer produced in ribosome; tumour produces fewer/no blood cells; tumour receives less/no nutrients/oxygen; required for growth of tumour/production of new cancer cells. **[4 marks: 1 mark for each explanation]**

03·1 **Any four from**: SSRI molecule blocks serotonin transport molecule; resulting in more serotonin being present in synaptic cleft; therefore, more serotonin binds with receptor sites on post-synaptic membrane; which triggers more nerve impulses/action potentials in the neurone/has an excitatory response; this stimulates centres of the brain associated with mood. **[4 marks: 1 mark for each explanation]**

03·2 Pre-cursor increase results in greater amount of dopamine **[1 mark]**; Increased dopamine excites areas of the brain involved in motor control/muscle movement **[1 mark]**.

03·3 **Any two from**: vesicles release more dopamine; less dopamine reabsorbed into pre-synaptic membrane; more dopamine available to trigger impulses in post-synaptic membrane. **[2 marks: 1 mark for each explanation]**

03·4 **Any two from**: a single action potential may arrive at a synaptic knob; there may not be enough transmitter molecules being secreted into a cleft to cause an action potential to be generated; a series of action potentials arrive at the synapse to build up transmitter substances to reach the threshold; the neurone will now send an action potential. **[2 marks: 1 mark for each explanation]**

04·1 Antigen binding site **[1 mark]**

04·2 **Any two from**: binding site **specific** to **antigen** on pathogen (outer membrane); binds/locks on to the pathogen; pathogens clumped together (complement); pathogen's toxin neutralised. **[2 marks: 1 mark for each description]**

04·3 Measure colour density/use spectrophotometer or colorimeter **[1 mark]**; The amount of hydrolysis (colour change) is proportional to the amount of antigen (venom) present in the test sample **[1 mark]**.

04·4 Test different snake venom molecules/proteins with **the same** antibody/IgG **[1 mark]**; A positive reaction/complex formed indicates the antibody/anti-venom is effective **[1 mark]**.

04·5 **Any two from**: venom disrupts/breaks bonds holding polypeptide chain/fibrinogen in blood together; 3D/tertiary structure lost; molecule unravels/globular structure becomes long chain; chains tangle/link together and precipitate/coagulate. **[2 marks: 1 mark for each suggestion]**

04.6 **Any two from:** a food **vacuole** is formed around the pathogen; hydrolytic **enzymes** from **lysosomes**/lysosomes join with food vacuole/reference to phagosome; enzymes digest/destroy pathogen. **[2 marks: 1 mark for each description]**

05.1 (Low) density **[1 mark]**

05.2 **Any two from:** plastic fibre content is much greater in sub-tidal regions than in estuarine or sandy regions; estuarine fibre concentration is greater than sandy; error bars do not overlap, so this difference is significant. **[2 marks: 1 mark for each conclusion]**

05.3 **Maximum of one from:** production of synthetic fibres shows a general trend of increase from the 1960s to the 1990s; there have been temporary, small dips in production on three occasions during this time period.

Maximum of two from: concentration of fibres greatest in 1980s; however – error/standard deviation bars in the two decades overlap considerably, so this might not be significant/any quoted comparison of data, e.g. fibre concentration in 1980s 0.045 per m^3 compared with 0.035 per m^3 in 1990s. **[3 marks: 1 mark for each explanation]**

05.4 To see if different organisms had different uptake rates **[1 mark]**; There is a range of feeding types **[1 mark]**.

05.5 **Any two from:** plastic fibres are not toxic in and of themselves; no evidence from this study that shows toxic substances are given off the fibres; there is no evidence for further accumulation of fibres further up the food chain/in consumers of these organisms. **[2 marks: 1 mark for each point made]**

05.6 **Any two from:** bioaccumulation/biomagnification; concentration of toxins increases further up the food chain where vertebrates tend to be found; toxins are persistent. **[2 marks: 1 mark for each explanation]**

05.7 Stated concentrations of PCBs are higher in liver **[1 mark]**; But standard deviations overlap in each organ category **[1 mark]**; Therefore may not be significant **[1 mark]**.

06 **Essay 1, ideal response, which would achieve 25 marks:**

Global warming causes a rise in average ambient temperatures. This masks the effects in specific climates and particular species, as the temperature changes in some situations can be profound and varied. Mean temperatures in some latitudes may actually go down due to the effect on weather systems. The effects on organisms can be grouped into those that have a physiological basis and those that operate on an ecological or macro level, although the two are very much connected.

In terms of physiology, a change in ambient temperature has a marked effect on ectotherms (organisms whose core temperature depends on the environment), but even endotherms (e.g. mammals and birds) will be affected to a certain degree, despite them having some control of body temperatures via homeostasis. In general terms, an organism's rate of metabolism will increase due to the effect of increased temperature.

Higher temperatures mean that the kinetic energy of molecules is greater. Therefore, enzyme activity increases (up to an optimum point) as there are more collisions per second between enzymes and their substrate molecules. This means that all reactions in the bodies of organisms will be affected, from digestion to respiration.

In plants, rate of photosynthesis is known to increase with temperature as the reactions that constitute the process rely on enzyme control. This increase is limited as, at temperatures above 40 °C, other factors such as carbon dioxide concentration or light intensity act as limiting factors.

As respiration rate also increases with temperature, then activity of ectotherms is affected. Such organisms may need to migrate or alter their behaviour to withstand extremes of hot or cold.

Decomposition has the process of respiration at its centre, thus bacteria and fungi will have increased metabolism, meaning rates of decay increase. This has implications for ecological niches (see later).

Movement of materials across cell membranes, whether they are molecules, ions or atoms, will also increase in rate as the processes depend on kinetic energy. Higher kinetic energy increases rates of diffusion in particular, which has implications for gaseous exchange and transpiration. In higher animals, increased temperature causes a shift to the left of the oxygen dissociation curve of haemoglobin. This means that less oxygen is unloaded due to an increased affinity for the haemoglobin.

In water, availability of oxygen will be lower as high temperatures increase the release of gases in solution. This may affect the survival and distribution of aquatic animals sensitive to oxygen concentration, e.g. stonefly nymphs and fish.

In general, ectotherms, e.g. reptiles, will be more active during the daytime. Behavioural adaptations such as exposure to the heat of the Sun will keep their metabolism at optimum conditions, which, in turn, makes them more competitive with endotherms. Other physiological effects in the bodies of endotherms include the effect on nervous transmission in receptors and neurones. In terms of thermo-regulation, the hypothalamus is more likely to trigger impulses to effectors, which increase sweating and vasodilation.

In plants, transpiration is accelerated at higher temperatures because evaporation, and hence diffusion of water from the spongy mesophyll cells in the leaf (and its loss through the stomata), increases. This in turn draws more water up through xylem cells as a result of the cohesion of water molecules. In high-temperature regimes, xerophytic adaptations become more predominant, such as leaves having reduced surface area to volume ratio (like cacti), or rolled-up leaves and sunken stomata. Higher temperatures are therefore acting as a selective pressure on plants.

All the above physiological effects influence the wider behaviour and ecology of organisms. For example, microbe decomposers (i.e. saprophytes) increase in number as the rates at which cells divide is increased. In terms of the carbon cycle, more carbon dioxide is released as aerobic respiration goes up. This in turn increases global warming as it is a greenhouse gas.

Unpredictable temperature changes cause migration or extinction of species. This will disrupt food webs due to new mixes of species and different interactions in terms of competition and predation. Populations that were once cohesive will become more isolated geographically, which in turn drives speciation and therefore evolution (see later).

In plants, temperature changes reduce biodiversity as fewer species are adapted for hot, dry climates. Despite increases in photosynthesis rate, the loss of so many plant species will reduce productivity, meaning fewer habitats and food for the animals that depend on them. As population numbers decrease this also has the effect of shrinking the gene pool. The lower range of genetic types make populations more vulnerable to environmental conditions and increase the frequency of harmful recessive alleles.

Selection pressures on higher animals would cause less hair and a leaner body with a higher surface area to volume ratios for rapid heat loss. So, ultimately, increased global temperatures will markedly affect the direction of evolution in the whole biosphere.

Essay 2, ideal response, which would achieve 25 marks:

Water is a major component of all cells. Movement of substances dissolved or suspended in this liquid is a vital necessity for all organisms. Single-celled organisms such as protists have no mass flow system and therefore rely on one or more of the following: diffusion, osmosis, active transport and facilitated diffusion. It should also be recognised that these processes may work alongside each other in the multicellular state.

All organisms are bounded by a phospholipid bilayer through which materials must pass. Moreover, eukaryotic cells contain membrane-bound organelles such as mitochondria and ribosomes. These present another barrier to movement of substances but also allow compartmentalisation of materials inside organelles, and the ability to carry out chemical reactions isolated from other interfering agents. Cell membranes are selectively permeable, meaning that they allow some substances through but not others.

Diffusion and its other form – facilitated diffusion – account for much of the movement across membranes and can occur directly through the membrane's lipid bilayer provided the substances are either lipid-soluble (i.e. hydrophobic), e.g. steroids, or very small, e.g. water, oxygen or carbon dioxide.

Diffusion is the movement of particles in a liquid or gas from a region of high concentration to one of low concentration. An example in the human body is gas exchange in the alveoli. Adult human lungs have a total area of around 100 m². This illustrates an important principle that diffusion is far more effective when there is a high surface area to volume ratio. The folded nature of the alveoli provides this. In addition, the single layer of cells in the alveolar membrane and capillary endothelium provide a short diffusion pathway, which also increases diffusion rate.

Facilitated diffusion is the movement of substances across a membrane through trans-membrane protein molecules spanning the whole phospholipid bilayer. The transport proteins are largely specific for one molecule, which means that substances can only cross a membrane containing the correct protein.

As with simple diffusion, the process is passive; therefore, no energy is expended and substances move down their concentration gradients. There are two kinds of transport protein: channel proteins, which form a water-filled pore or channel in the membrane; and carrier proteins that possess a binding site for a specific solute and repeatedly change between two states. This makes the site alternately open on opposite sides of the membrane. The substance will bind on the side where it is at a high concentration and be released where it is at a low concentration. Examples of substances that use this mode of transport include glucose and amino acids.

Glucose is a hydrophilic monosaccharide and cannot diffuse directly through the hydrophobic membrane. Specific extrinsic glucose channel proteins have a complementary shape that allows glucose to enter the cytoplasm by facilitated diffusion down a concentration gradient. This absorption of glucose is stimulated by the presence of insulin produced from the pancreatic cells.

Occasionally, carrier proteins have two binding sites and can carry two molecules at once. This is called cotransport, e.g. the sodium/glucose cotransporter found in the small intestine.

A special case of diffusion is osmosis. The contents of cells contain solutions of many different solutes, and each solute molecule attracts water molecules in a hydration shell. The more concentrated the solution, the more solute molecules there are in a certain volume, and consequently the more water molecules included in the hydration shell. This means that there are fewer free water molecules to diffuse easily across the membrane of a cell. The overall effect of this is that the net movement of water occurs down its concentration gradient, or in other words, from a dilute solute concentration to a more concentrated one. Putting it another way, water moves down a water potential gradient.

There are many examples where this occurs between plant cells, e.g. in the mesophyll of the leaf. Here, the dilution of cell contents as water moves into the cell raises the water potential, thus enabling water to move on into the next cell and so on. In the mammalian kidney, osmosis accounts for the re-absorption of water from the collecting duct. Here, sodium ions in the medulla act as the solute, effectively drawing the water out of the collecting duct and back into the capillaries.

Active transport is where pumping of substances takes place across a membrane via a trans-membrane protein pump molecule. The protein binds a molecule of a substance to one side of the membrane, then changes shape and releases it on the other side. These proteins are very specific; therefore, a different protein pump exists for each transported molecule. The protein pumps are ATPase enzymes. The splitting of ATP into ADP and phosphate as catalysed by this enzyme releases energy to change the shape of the protein pump. This means that active transport requires the release of energy and is the only transport mechanism that can transport substances against a concentration gradient. An example of active transport is in root hair cells where mineral ions such as nitrate and potassium ions are absorbed from the soil against a concentration gradient.

Movement of molecules within a cell occurs from organelle to organelle, e.g. in respiration, pyruvate produced from glycolysis, moves from the cytoplasm into the mitochondrial matrix. Here, it is a reactant in the Krebs cycle and produces reduced NAD and FAD co-enzymes. These then diffuse to the cristae where they pass their electrons down an electron transport chain in a series of redox reactions. Similar transport of hydrogen ions within chloroplasts occurs during the light independent reaction of photosynthesis. This process is termed chemiosmosis.

Larger molecules, such as messenger RNA, can migrate from the nucleus to the ribosomes in order to manufacture polypeptides in the process of translation. Although larger than the water molecule, mRNA is still small enough to diffuse out through the nuclear pores and bind to ribosomes on the rough endoplasmic reticulum.

Further specific examples of movement across membranes are nervous conduction and the setting up of action potentials in receptors and neurones. Here, the small potential is generated by the influx of sodium ions through a sodium-potassium pump. Additionally, synaptic transmission requires the diffusion of a neurotransmitter between neurones at the nerve junction.

We can therefore see that movement of substances is a basic requirement of life, and can be achieved by varied means that result in a high degree of control.

Essay 1: guide to the allocation of marks

Specification reference	Topic area
3.1.4	Enzymes and their function [2 marks]
3.2.3	Movement across cell membranes [2 marks]
3.3.1	Effect of SA/Vol ratio [1 mark]
3.3.2	Gas exchange and oxygen concentration in water [1 mark]
3.3.4.1	Temperature's effect on haemoglobin [1 mark]
3.3.4.2	Transpiration and diffusion rates of water vapour from leaves [2 marks]
3.4.4	Genetic diversity and adaptation [2 marks]
3.4.6	Biodiversity [2 marks]
3.5.1	Rates of photosynthesis [2 marks]
3.5.2	Rates of respiration [2 marks]
3.5.4	Effect of temperature on rate of decomposition [1 mark]
3.6.2.1	Effect of temperature on speed of conductance along neurones [1 mark]
3.6.4.1	Homeostasis and control of body temperature [2 marks]
3.7.3	Speciation (geographic isolation) [1 mark]
3.7.4	Migration of organisms and issues relating to the conservation of species and habitats [3 marks]

Essay 2: guide to the allocation of marks

Specification reference	Topic area
3.1.7	Water [1 mark]
3.1.8	Inorganic ions [2 marks]
3.2.3	Transport across cell membranes [6 marks]
3.3.1	Surface area to volume ratio [1 mark]
3.3.2	Gas exchange [2 marks]
3.3.3	Digestion and absorption [2 marks]
3.5.1	Photosynthesis [2 marks]
3.5.2	Respiration [2 marks]
3.6.1.2	Receptors [1 mark]
3.6.2.1	Nerve impulses [2 marks]
3.6.2.2	Synaptic transmission [1 mark]
3.6.3	Skeletal muscles [1 mark]
3.6.4.2	Control of blood glucose concentration [1 mark]
3.6.4.3	Control of blood water potential [1 mark]